CANTOS

ALFRED ARTEAGA

▼ ▼

Acknowledgements

Some of the poems have appeared in: Berkeley Poetry Review, Blue Mesa Review, Byzantium, Irvine Chicano Literary Prize 1985-87, New Chicano Writing, Quarry West.

Cover Art : "Alerta"
Yreina Cervántez

Graphic Design and Typography:
Hiram Durán Alvarez

ISBN: 0-9624536-2-5
Printed in the United States

CHUSMA HOUSE PUBLICATIONS

Para mis hijas

ફ્~

▼▼

Contents

▼ ▼

X antecanto: the xicano sign

These cantos chicanos begin with X and end with X. They are examples of xicano verse, verse marked with the cross, the border cross of alambre y río, the cross of Jesus X in Native America, the nahuatl X in méxico, mexicano, xicano. It is our mark, our cross, our X, our sign of never ceasing being born at the point of two arrows colliding, X, and at the gentle laying of one line over another line, X. It is the sound we make to mark one and other, August 29, familia, raza, as well as to exclude ourselves from the patterns of death imposed from without. We sign the X each time we speak we cross at least one border. And because it is our sign andamos cruzando cruzados, naciendo siendo xicanos otra vez, cada vez, esta vez. I am the point of my own X but the arms, los brazos vienen de lejos, and the arms reach far.

Nacido, East Los X3; Escribo, San Jo X4: AA

PRIMERO

Arrival

First, the island.
The cross of truth.
Another island.
A continent.
A line, half water, half metal.

An island of birds, "Ccollanan."
An island of birds,
"Ccollanan Pachacutec!"
Sounds above an island, in
the air, trees, "Ccollanan Pachacutec!"
Female sounds. "Ricuy
anceacunac yahuarniy richacaucuta!"
An island of female birds, imagine
the sounds, the air, the trees, at times
the silence, the slither in thorns.

So perfect a shape, right
angles, the globe yields to so
straight a line, look. One
line, zenith to nadir, heaven,

precipitation. The only other,
straighter still than that horizon
we see at sea, perfect: paradise.
That horizontal line, from
old to new, he knew would yield,
yes, so perfect a move, he
knew, yes, so perfect a shape
yes.

Trees caught his thoughts.
Birds and onshores brought them
from the boats. She knew those
thoughts, heard those songs.
Could there be one more island?
Birds, sounds, perhaps pearls,
gold? Eden-Guanahaní, perhaps
another? "O my Marina, my new
found island. License my roaving
hands, and let them go, before,
behind, between, above, below."
West.

América, América. Feminine
first name, continent named
for him. América.
Here, Santa Fe. Here, the true
faith. I claim, in the name of
the father. Land of thorns,
in the name of the son.

The edge of this world
and the other, is marked
in water: ocean, river, wave to
her, she waits on the other
side. Aquí, se llama la Juana,
de apellido Juárez, india,
prieta y chaparra, la que le encanta
al gringo, al gachupín.

Island of cactus, genus
Cuauhtémoc. Island of rose,
land of thorns. Pedro de
Alvarado, an eagle, la
región transparente, a
night of smoke. Marina
Nightear, an ocean contained
in one woman, as it was in
the beginning, world
without end, fallen
eagle.

So feminine a shape. So female
a bay. Another shape: gliding
birds. Another: touching trees.
True name of woman, Vera Cruz,
body of woman. "He named me
Xochitepec, yes so we are all flowers

of the mountain, all a woman's body,
that was one true thing he said in
his life." Above, birds,
leaves, above so woman a form.
Las quince letras: not the seven words:
Contestó Malintzin, "yes
I said yes I will Yes."

En el nombre
de la Virgen de las Espinas,
ella que en buen ora nasco,
this archeology is born: here
tibia, here ball courts, codices,
teeth. Inside, the caves are
painted. Here is an architecture,
see, toco, toco,
tocotín:

Tla ya timohuica,
totlazo Zuapilli,
maca ammo, Tonantzin,
titechemoilcahuíliz.
Mati itlatol ihiyo
Huel ni machicáhuac
no teco qui mati.

En la sangre, en las espinas
de la Virgen de Santa Fe,
these names are written:
América Estados-Unidos, née
México. I name her
Flower of the Mountain,
Coatepec-Cihuatepec-Cuicatepec
Amor Silvestre,
Terra Nova,
Cuerpo de Mujer.

The edge of this world
and the other, is marked
in metal: on this side America,
on this side América.
Nights they spill from
San Diego and Los Angeles
threading the steel mesh
como nada, los verdaderos
alambristas, buscando el cuerpo
de mujer, buscando,
Xochitepec.

SEGUNDO

Textos vivos

En lo negro that is blackness,
en lo negro, that negritude,
in that night sheet sin
cloud sin moon sky, en lo negro, cielo
vivo
in that black sheet stretched
from one hand a un autre
este negro ósculo
oscuro de papel manantial
de mano a mano que ves
esta vez, Je est,
yes, in that yes blank sin
blanco, black held in your now
hand hear hand, aquí, mano vocal,
you see yes, que ves esta vez, negro
vivo
que ves, que lees, el negro que lees,
ahora que lees, aquí que lees,
en el negro que lees, ahora y aquí
que lees el pecado sin negro
vivo

Entre las manos extiendes la red
from one hand to the other que lees,
desde una mano, one to another,
la red extiende, hoja colorada no
suelta, la red extendida y colorada
from one hand to the other que ves,
l'outre-vie du texte, outre-texte,
que lees, la red que detienes
al momento, that you read
entre estas dos manos
vivas
aquel color del filo, aquellas
marcas también, that you
hold from one hand tú que
ves, tú who reads this instant,
that color del filo there you
see, know you see there red, sí you
read en aquellas rojas marcas
vivas
extended red, color of solstice
that moment only, red solo, red
color that instant, manos escritas,
extendiendo lo rojo, red color of
manuscript soltice,
tú, tú que lees el estreno
nuevamente rojo, this only soltice,
rojoglífico, color that you read,
from hand, tu mano a esa obra,
rojo you read, aquí, enfrente las

hojas estrechas, no sueltas,
vivas

Here it is, the equinox, next to
the hand's skin, beside the other's
too, que ves desocupado
lector, inexplicablemente
despierto, la red negra, la hoja roja:
the black that is silence, letter,
the red that is on, syllable,
negroglífico, rojezcrito, here
it is lying between your hands
alive red alive black, here
it is next to and beside lies
alife

Negrita, Red Man,
de isla y continente
brilliant skins, bright red,
bright black:
hope, splendor, mirror.
Ella, la California, es la serga
de Esplandián, hija
ilegítima de la amada de jaula.
Y él, el bravo Californio, niño perdido,
nuevamente salido y producido,
de aquellas vivas llamas y cenizas,
del ardentísimo y Christianísimo Filipo
que pues en Nueva México quiso ver fénix.

Terra Nova:
hope, splendor, mirror. Bright
back, reflecting, tezcatl,
reflect, nechichauallano,
mirror: A new island of pearls
in the black hands of women; a new
continent of men blood colored::

tlilli in quecholli
tlilli in tlapalli
in ixochiuh in xronotopxopan
xiuhtlacuilolli ya amoxcalitec
krugozory:
xicancuicatl

TERCERO

El viaje

White, from white Mictlan, south,
to Xopan, to Tenochtitlan,
"Nosotros descendimos hasta
el río impasible, nosotros de piel
roja, buscando la señal: una isla
en las montañas, en las nubes
claras de águilas, la serpiente
despeñada, el nopal antípoda.
A una isla mixtitlan, a la isla mixtitlan,
dimos el nombre
Isla Xochitepec."
From Aztlan, the word made motion,
tentli, yollotl, yolotia,
to eagle, to snake, to cactus,
each black.

Old man, conquistador,
Bavieca, Tizón and Colada,
father of Coyote, Chamizo,

Sambaigo and Combujo,
father of Lobo, of Barquino,
of Mulato, father of Mestizo.
"From Europe's cold black waters
to Tepeyac, Flower of the Mountain,
where sad children shall kneel
before us. In the name of Our Lady
of the Thorns, we shall baptize a
Juan-Diego Oxomoco, a Marina Nightear,
baptize a María Castellano Cortés,
a Rodrigo Río-Bravo."
And west, dark
women and pearls. "Esplandián!
Plus Ultra, Esplandián!"
Old words made blood,
old words made
new.

Many mothers, a father who
loosed dogs one sad night,
feathers from the quetzal, a
bird who now coos in Spanish.
From the high plateau, from a
gulf town, across desert to one
river, half water, half metal. A
mesh of steel and spray, only
threaded by the mad. Railroads

to the madness, highways to the
cities of the mad, and a boat.
"J'ai rêvé le fleuve m'a laissé
descendre où je voulais." In
my dream, a woman approaches
the fence, she offers mezcal,
there is something
dead in the liquid, we
drink from the common bottle,
our skins are the same
color, in the darkness
agave and mesquite
seem one.

Lone star, bear flag,
Fredonia.
Sea to shining ore.
To San Antonio, Santa Fe,
Monterey. To Tijuana or Juarez
Saturday night, border
Chapultepec: young girls
descend, unfurl to drunken
gringos, las heroicas, "Viva
el pinche dólar."Chapultepec,
grasshopper hill: a park
devoted to the pleasure of
marines, devoted to

grasshoppers. Three brown
girls of age stroll by, their color
flagrant.
Long live the land
of plenty.

"If I could fly from this
island of clouds, from this
green island of clouds, from
this green island of orange
men lions, not follow
for long months, like cattle or
breaking sea on reef.
All exiles are kings' sons, after all.
Sad Tara. Leaden sea. Bright heavens."
To Canada, America, Churubusco,
Chapultepec. Flight of John Riley.
Harp of Erin, a Shamrock, a green field.
Was it Col. Bennet Riley or was
it Capt. O'Shay? 16 hanged at
San Angel, April 9, 1847. 4 hanged
at Mixcoac, April 10. 30 hanged
at Chapultepec, grasshopper hill,
where the children heroes took
flight, April 13. The rest: 50 lashes,
an iron collar with 3 prongs, 6
inches, 8 pounds each; a head shaving;

a D branded on the cheek.
From green Tara island to
green Tenochtitlan island,
from Erin to Aztlan,
I remember,
then.

Primero, el poder y la palabra. Napoleón
o el poder del pasado, Juárez o
el poder de la raza. Entre las
dos orillas del poder, un puente:
Carlota, que convierte
la historia de ambos poderes
en teatro. Habla la Hapsburg,
"J'aurais voulu montrer aux
enfants ces dorades, ces serpents
emplumés, cette pyramide. Les
mexicains ont bercé mes détrades,
et d'ineffables ventes m'ont ailée
par instants. Ce pays sauvage,
ce bateau perdu."
Encore

QUARTO

Xronotop Xicano

Aguila negra, rojo chante.
Tinta y pluma.
Textos vivos,
written people: the vato
with la vida loca on his neck,
the vata with p.v., the ganga with
tears, the shining cross. Varrio
walls: codices; storefront
placazos: varrio names,
desafíos, people names.
Written cars, names etched
in glass, "Land of a Thousand
Dances." Placas
and love etched in schools.

Faces of Indians branded
by Spaniards.
Faces of Irishmen branded

by Americans.
Gachupín: he who kicks
with the boot.
Yankee: new man, of the
new world, Yancuic.
Xicano: cantador, namer.

xicancuicatl
floricanto
canto
canto

Santa Cruz, 1986

5

Romance Blanco

There is the man who comes to the door, to
the nine year old girl, "I," does not know him.
No, "No," he puts his foot to the door, kicks,
Her eye, her hand, her nine year leg too waits.
He claims he wants to eat food, "I am nine,
but can talk to a man whose foot breaks here:
the door is mine." This wall, the whole house too.
No one here will give you food. Nor will I.

His boots come from Spain. He has the steel of
his trade at his side. Eyes stare, but no tongue
speaks, "No," or "Sí." A nine year old girl stands
still, "I can speak 'No' for man, for him whose
name claims me, 'No' for the one I come from
but can't talk to you man whose foot breaks now.
The voice is mine." This word, the whole word too.
He leaves. Old, dust, smoke-blood, empty dead time.

6

Corrido Blanco

Her notebook declares, "If for you fathers
my logos suffers too, (what did Paul say?)
'Mulieres' You 'in Ecclesia tace-
ant.' Too, mujeres en iglesia, you

te nacen, palabrita, tú, mía."
In the schools from Rome, you are born living,
from London too: nace la palabra.
And you become and kill a tongue or two.

Criolla, woman whose words I see, hear,
maestra, teacher, eye and ear and tongue
for me. Here I am one nine year old boy.
No hay razón, sólo poder. Here I

hear, see, palabra suya, "Know: children
be silent in school. No language, or word
or sound you know from homelands. Ameri-
ca, no way to spell it but one. I know."

Houston-Santa Cruz, 1988

7

NW6

How many degrees whiter
north? How dead into the
dead land: Mictlan:
white, north, far land,
in the quiet and still white
whisper of faint death?
Northern, northern land.

Yet what is the color that transforms words
and names from breathing beasts and human
beings with arms and blood and children too?

What does Tupac Amarú say, does
Cuauhtémoc say, does
Lolita Lebrón have to say?

"Green island,
'Black Island'."
Broken in(to) lands, bones in
black & white X-rays.

And if the northern northern land were
not so edged in bleak seas nor so
alone, the sad birds did not freeze
in cavern streets and break like stone
in rare shade, what then? Would

it collect the voice of the dead in
choir and give rein to chant so
lonely and keen a wail, that it could
make me forget?
Or remember that in the land of
the dead, the dead breed faster than we
can guess, having sex by memory, more
than we can do?

Oh Mictlan, northern land,
white one death,
bank and hue of time stretched thin,
what then?

8

muñeca, muñequita

muñeca de paja
muñequita
hecha de paja
muñequita
no tienes nada
muñequita
nomás la paja
muñequita

qué vas a ser
cuando crezcas
en el verano
de año que entra
mamá o
muchachita
o quedas paja
muñequita

8

world-echo, little world-echo

world-echo on the page
little world-echo
ambiguous page
little world-echo
no tender nothing
little world-echo
names on the page
little world-echo

why was a lord
wandering crazy
in the veranda
but did not enter
mother of
so much and so little
on the dearest page
little world-echo

9

The Small Sea of Europe

At the end of the eighteenth century, Hindu law, insofar
as it can be described as a unitary system, operated in
terms of four texts that "staged" a four-part episteme
defined by the subject's use of memory: *sruti* (the
heard), *smriti* (the remembered), *sastra* (the learned-
from-another), and *vyavahara* (the performed-in-
exchange).

—Gayatri Chakravorty Spivak

In Europe's small sea,
a system of exchange:
forms of life
and motion in sign.

The Case In Point–

Verkehr:
'the motion of women, of slaves,

in sleekcongested automobiles, trunks
with drugs'

Verkehr,
from the Sanscrit, (small sea),
vyavahara:
'performance traffic,
former act of transformation,
an exchange.'
Ecos escritos: *Sruti, Smriti, Sastra*
three sisters in myth, very
sources of Europe, Western Man,
the very sounds slipping: 3Ss, sans(é)crit
3Ss:
3Ss: ecos escritos (S grito)

Again, then.
Verkehr:
S_1 in the automobile beside S_2, S_3
at the wheel, 'Sister...' furtive, slave-like
movements (escape? from/to what/where?)
But who can drive? Of course, S_2 remembers,
tells, S_1 hears, inserts the key,
demonstrates, S_3 learns, starts the motor: of
course, escape, With-Drugs o wild & steering slave

through furtive traffic, changing lanes, exchanging
places of courses, escape:
Sruti hears, Smriti recalls, Sastra learns from an   other:
S drive and drive, verkehr
S *verkehr:* vyavahara
a performance, vyavahara,
the S sound of abandon.

(Or) Again:
Sastra (née 'furtive slave') learned
furtive from
Sruti: (née 'furtive slave') heard
furtive from
Smriti (née 'furtive slave') remembers
furtive from
the small sea of history, the big C of capital,
first squirt of legend, trancendental quill
and myth-inks, rib stain here first
no ear, no hearing, across which sheets first
defined smear.

I remember Smriti, in the dictionary,
Verkehr:
'fast women in cars escape with drugs'
like Texas, but this is Berlin
to Paris, night rides hard riding off course

3 woman Ss written off across this old sad continent
fast esses, stained-fast essences, the Ss senses (S sense)
of woman defi(l/n)ed.

Some big *Dichtung*
this place,
a ce.

London, 1988

10

A mon seul désir
5.2.89

La brisa, la frialdad
de aquel domingo en París,
día húmedo: yo recuerdo como
las meras piedras de la calle
murmuraban esas sílabas sibilantes
en tiempo con tus pies, mis pies
por el paseo antiguo de París
por la tarde.
Te veo todavía, tú, mujer
de otro tiempo, de visiones,
tú valoras los sentidos que todavía
actualizan esta tela vital. ¿Cuáles
animales franceses te revelan hoy
día y a la ánima perceptible ese día pasado, allí en París?
Había sonidos desvanecidos, ese domingo,
de un nivel más elevado que el de piedra,
más líquido y tenue: ya oigo y no oigo ya.
Si pudiéramos hablar, estuviéramos hablando,
en el momento actual, (pero, sí, ¿cuál momento, qué texto?)
¿que no nos pararíamos nosotros mismos,
y no oiríamos, una vez más, este sonido brutal
y el eco ajeno, dos rasgos tejidos
de la noche parisiense?
Y en fin, se nota tu boca presente
y el parto de las notas afines, ausente,

¿tu palabra, tal como tu sonido?
  si parisílabos los
  dos, parisílabos, sí

Oigo:

«Un miedo que tengo, de no sé qué, me persigue, me
plasma, forma ambos emociones y modos, el miedo que
es mi texto y el preámbulo mío. ¿Qué no? Yo no sé ni
quién soy, ni para qué, para quién soy, ni estoy, esta tarde
en París, día húmedo, día antiguo, perfectamente mío, día
mío, París, vía antigua, avenida a la calle. Cómo me
asustan estas huellas: el palimpsesto parisiense,
esfumado, muy esfumado; la paleta diurnal y desteñida;
la acuarela que pertenece al invierno débil y pálido; todos
de la tarde perdida, la tela ajena y tejida. Y a veces me
asusta el color de algo, tal sonido de tal animal, por
ejemplo, la ausencia tuya o la humedad del paseo visto
por mi parte, por el punto de vista mío. ¿Qué no me
asusta? Así como digo yo, así, así me sigue, sin son, pero
así. Y así yo recuerdo los animales que pintarrajaban
ellos mismos en las piedras, digo paredes, de tal pueblo,
no me acuerdo el nombre, ni cómo se llama ¿te acuerdas?
sí, de seguro. ¿Cuántos pequeños rasgos contiguos a las
veredas y vaderas antiguas? ¿Cuántas marcas, manchas y
rastras persistentes? como te explico así. Quizás en la
tarde de un día de invierno por ejemplo, oirás, entre los
edificios antiguos de París por una tarde húmeda, día
húmedo, como es, un eco tan
desconocido, como te digo, que si fuera
posible, nunca más dormirías.

»Ya sí, así, animal doloroso, rasgar y derramar para siempre hasta siempre, así, que sí. Yo recuerdo cuando (y antes que) oigo, porque nunca oigo sin recordar o haber recordado antes, aquella memoria, imagen y pánico, día doloroso como escribo yo, Pluma y Tinta: mi animal, animal mío, persigue, domingo mío, entre las ramblas antiguas de París, escritas por la tarde, día y agua, agua y animal, París mío.

»O animal claro de huella y presencia, cuerpo de agua de piedra de brisa, animal que asoma, con hebras rojas y negras y un azul tan profundo que debe significar, que me asombra, que me pasma a mí: Por mis calles de mi pueblo, de mi tiempo de mis aguas, por el tiempo, por lo bueno hasta siempre hasta siempre. O animal, por los míos, miedo y garra de la vida cotidiana: ¿qué y qué pues? ¿En qué forma? la próxima vez, esta vez, por mi tarde, París tan tarde. O pueblo mío, el susto precisa la mancha, el rasgo nunca aclara, ¿letra y humo significan todavía, hoy día? Día de agua. ¿Tú y yo? Cuáles animales se mueven por mis calles día tras día, tras día, y no imagino de la noche, París, pueblo antiguo, marea de susto, animal herido, animal mío, día de fiesta, día que se inmuta, día corto de invierno, débil, dominguito día 7.»

¿La tinta? ¿Dónde y cuándo quedará?
¿Nace en la luz, la paleta, la pluma,
o alrededor del órgano de la vista?
Literalmente no es una metáfora,
la franja y las hebras del ojo.
Pero ¿en qué consiste un color
que mete y sale, sometiéndose a
un orden solitario, distinto,

una tela imponiéndose entre
la piedra y el tacto húmedo? ¿Verde,
la franja tal como las hebras?
Es una dirección pura,
una trayectoria de huellas nomás;
es una locución hablada con
temor, vista por alguien.
Aquí la brisa anima
el discurso fabricado y el respiro brutal.
El pueblo de colores bajos y mates
se trasluce en tintas y hebras claras y matizadas.
El día de varios verdes
desborda la fábrica del eco
que eres y que quedas, tú, mujer, aquí
en tu antiguo París.
Fíjate.
El pájaro no es nada, un son gastado.
Los pies hacen el ruido, las trazas, la vista.
Tú asomas, tejes el sonido y el son
con la brisa y la frialdad del momento de mi,
digo, de nuestro domingo.

Una niña entra y sale una maravilla.
O mejor, se trazuma por la tela
que es París por la tarde,
una persona.
Milagro ¿qué no?

Paris, 1989

11

Rocamador, Asleep

What trains cross
the night childhood
each stop passing still.

Barcelona, 1989

12

Letters of Color

No existe el amanecer. No existe el atardecer. El sol mismo ha muerto.
Sólo quedan las nubes. Absolutas. Verdes.

—Juan Felipe Herrera

                                   each
green eye in a heaven of blue, a fistfull
of understanding

—Lorna Dee Cervantes

Verde no eres tú

—Rosario Castellanos

"Green is most sad.
Germany is this color
and shines
this temperature
always…"
        —she writes
me in letters. What
could she mean, these

words this breath, these
proofs of woman
to me?
The letters, of course, I know
are not her:
She is not the green. Yet,
because she writes,
I write too. This is true.

So
I collect green: a rain forest monkey
hides there in tree, I see it; that whale breathes
a cold and broken green, passes the
California point; one green follows the sad
goodbye before the same old sleep,
I get it; bland pages enfold my (for now
I lay claim) color; and the green
I find forged in cannon and fatigue;
these greens
I gather.

But I do not visit Germany, despite
the joy of aluminum for gold,
I can't. Can her letters contain this?
I hold now, this very instant, in
my own hands, the saddest color,
the most Germanic green. Things I
have gathered with my own hands, things
encased in green, essentially green and

things seemingly green to any eye,
I hold. And
because she breathes,
I breathe too. Or this I lie.

I understand primate refuge in trees,
understand migration again
and again past the whaling town
site of slaughter, offal still I'm sure.
I know all the German glyphs like
lines which crease my hands,
I know them.

Yet letters come to me in breath almost
still, she does not tell me more than sad.
I am left only with weapons,
stupidly useless this second. She
writes. I am left with hands full of dumb
color, hands of useless speech that says no
thing, less.
This woman who writes sad green
colors me painted bird
wings before my eyes.

I have made children, planted trees.
I have killed men. I write these words.
My hands are green, I don't know
what it means.

Coyoacán, el otoño gris

Querido Alfredo—

*Triste, verde y alemán fue la letra desaparecida de mi
nombre—ojo—te mando una última letra: ausente,
la tehuana-mexicana; presente, el mexicano-chicano.
Escríbeme en caló, escribo, en color.*

—Frida

13

Canto Pacífico

From my house I can see the widest sea
Pacific blue-black, green, and slate.
White where it breaks rock and
sprays on breeze, and almost
true black at night in fog.
El mar pacífico, named in Spanish
in Panama, perhaps in English
too, Sea of Peace, peaceful pacific, the
ocean that could hold all other seas
in its bays and gulfs and streams alone.

Now,
from my wooden and landed house, above
the sandstone cliff, past the sand's
touch, I see the pacific ocean. It is my view,
my sound, at times my breath.
And I am drawn into the family
of pacific people, we share the widest sea, every

day we bare our feet, hurl hook and net,
light candles in the naves of our souls.
In morning ritual, we turn and reflect,
recognize one and other, pacific people.
From Santa Cruz, I extend my hand
south to Cabo San Lucas, and from there, a baker,
a young girl with worn shoes, a sailor who
spends his day wet with spray, people I have
yet to meet but whose words I know, in turn,
they extend their hands, old and worn
and new, to farther hands
along the coast.
This ocean rite is not known to others but pacific people.
I share it now with you land locked ones,
and you whose seas are smaller, more silent, numb.
Perhaps you'll come one day to taste
pacific salt and someone will touch
your hand with his, with hers,
with mine.

Then
the peace in spray and wave,
the crashing surf and storm, can touch
your pacific hand. Then, the wildest storm,
the ocean's most wild dance against
the sandstone cliffs of Santa Cruz, the wave's

brave pass, silent over the deep abyss
off Cabo San Lucas, will seem nothing,
nothing like the sparks of torture in pacific Chile,
hand cuffed to metal bed frames, shot with electricity;
nothing like that moment Victor Jara
is cut off from language, cut off
from his pacific hands too.
The biggest wave,
blue-black, green or slate, that rips
through kelp forest, tide pool, and wide
sand bar, that swells above your
head, that curls and crushes and makes
everything confusion, that wave
is nothing like one desaparecido,
in pacific Guatemala;
nothing at all like the wall
of desperate cries, desperate sleepless
nights, and desperate madness
that swells above, rips through, and crushes
wife, brother, lover, of the one disappeared,
nothing at all.
Not the degree of cold surf, in January or
August winter, that makes each bare
foot bone cry out and panic; not the
retreating wave, the riptide back
and out, that could, if it so desired,

take with it to its watery home, a house
of stone; and not the rising tide
that cuts off the cove's retreat, imagine
the fear this creates at night, no not even this;
is nothing, nothing at all
like one dollar's worth of bullet,
boot, or contra's bandage,
not one.

O Pacific ocean, océano pacífico,
at this moment, I leave poetry. I watch
your motion from my window, and scan
ceaseless lines of waves coming in, coming
in relentless peace.
Who thinks of me, this moment,
thinking of the sea? Peaceful
Pacific Ocean, not at all not peaceful.
I see, hear, now I breathe, breaking
now, peaceful lines of waves,
breaking lines
of peaceful waves.

Santa Cruz, 1990

14

Respuesta a Frida

11/1, X4

On n'est pas morte mais déjà presque vivante,
presque née, en train de naître peut-être, dans ce
passage hors frontière et hors temps qui caractérise
le désir. Désir de l'autre, désir du monde....
Traverser l'opacité du silence et inventer nos
existences, nos amours, là où il n'y a plus de
fatalité d'aucune sorte.

—Marie Uguay

Q. F.—

[*cctbc*, Frida,
y *ccsa* letra *tdg* a
kiss, a lacuna. Each
drop of letter, yes, is
a fall of sorts.

Socc. So cae cada
gota, some heaven
missed.

2 color: Frieda 2 Frida,
I write *2u* Frida las *2, at,*
cuata *d2* misma cuata,
cuerpo *d2* mismo cuerpo,
F-Kerida, ambas
Frida, la misma *d2*
misma, Frieda.
at, 1 última respuesta:
en la cuna de las letras vacías,
echo el son hueco de un huerco,
y tras la arena de tierra y tiempo,
se suelta tu eco]

I am sorry such time has passed since you dropped
me off that last letter. It is fall still in California
and so much frigid earth between us (el otoño gris,
Frida, California fría). I close my eyes as I write
now (te rías). I can see your brown eyes, your
brow, your row of black braids, *(O yes you're you,*
yet your own image becomes mine in my mind's eye,
becomes our own in the blank of the letter o yes) and
black snakes curve above your head.

—AA

▼▼

[Cuento
1 pierna, 1 ceja, 1 nacimiento,
2 Fridas, 3 ojos, unos picotazos, más sangre.
Menos 1 letra
(verde, el kalor alemán de Frieda la judía)
menos 1 letra
(trieste, la de una narrativa del único dolor posible
de andar quebrada en mala hora).
Encuentro
Frida menos la letra,
Frida, con una sola ceja, el plumado européo,
Frida la cuata tehuana, la cojita,
Frida menos la letra.]

P.S.—
"Se van como pájaros, de volada, like clumps of cut
hair, each strand and bird signifying great love."
Como cartas a los muertos and the soft clothing, buti
suave, of the loved one. And the sobres amarillos,
llenos de cartas llenas de letras de los desparecidos,
such yellow butterflies in the air about me como las
últimas letras de sexo, como s.

[la cuna vacía, sin son, sin *bb*,
2 las 2, parecidas, *2d* la letra
desaparecida, Frida, en fin,
d parte *d* mí, *atnlD.F.*, Q.F., desde
X4 today, this last letter, I write

"*Q.F.,*" florecida en caló. 2flor yo canto,
color de caló:
trieste, colorado, y de aztlán.]

Y en fin, *F,*
¿quién más falta la letra?
¿la poeta que ahora canta en caló, o
el pintor que miró un color
encarnado por los límites de todos los
ayeres, o
la lectora que apretará en las manos,
al acabar de leer, una vida literalmente
vaciada?

Just as,
venadita,
the eighteen letters = las quince letras,
we come *bbn*
la cuna of the letter.

San José-Chicago, 1990

15

For My Lady Going to War

It is true
man and all his stories
fill our speaking mouths with words,
sand so dry we can never spit it all out.
Our dreaming skulls cannot keep out
the constant pricking of old tales
but crack and break instead.
Our shadows are black
and thicken because so many
others have crossed this way before.
This is all too true.

But I swear
when our two bodies touch,
when my flesh and your flesh
wage the dance making life, the
gasp and grab like death,
there in the light of what we two do,
I am
one man
and I imagine you
one woman.

Berkeley, 1991

▼ ▼

"el Mundo iluminado, y yo despierta."

—*SJ de la X*

▼▼▼

Notes to Cantos

The Cantos are not spoken in silence, and some, especially los primeros, respond to echoes and recall voice in time with voice.

1.8, 10, 12 (Canto 1, Lines 8, 10, 12): Tupac Amarú, epigraph to part 3, "Los conquistadores," of Pablo Neruda's *Canto General.*

1.35-38: John Donne. Elegie XIX, "To His Mistris Going to Bed."

1.70-74, 77-8: James Joyce. "Penelope," *Ulysses.*

1.81: Gaspar Pérez de Villagrá. "Primer Canto," *La Historia de la Nueva México.*

1.88-94: Sor Juana Inés de la Cruz. *Asunción, 1676* and *San Pedro Nolasco, 1677.*

2.28: Marie Uguay. *l'outre-vie.*

2.73-77: Gaspar Pérez de Villagrá. "Primer Canto," *La Historia de la Nueva México.*

3.3-5, 22-25: Arthur Rimbaud. "Le bateau ivre."

3.31-32: Gaspar Pérez de Villagrá. "Primer Canto," *La Historia de la Nueva México.*

3.47-48: Arthur Rimbaud. "Le bateau ivre."

3/63-75: William Carlos Williams. "Sunday in the Park."

3.88, 89-97: *Stars and Stripes,* Mexico City, 1848.

3.103-109: Carlos Fuentes. *Todos los gatos son pardos.*

3.110-116: Arthur Rimbaud. "Le bateau ivre."

6.3-4: Sor Juana Inés de la Cruz. *Respuesta a Sor Filotea de la Cruz.*

9. Epigraph: Gayatri Chakravorty Spivak, "Can the Subaltern Speak?"

10. Title: "A mon seul désir," from the tapestry, Musée de Cluny.

12. Epigraphs: Juan Felipe Herrera, "Noche Verde Nuclear;" Lorna Dee Cervantes, "Meeting Mescalito at Oak Hill Cemetary;" Rosario Castellanos, "Poesía no eres tú."

14. Epigraph: Marie Uguay. *l'outre-vie.*

About the Author

Born in East Los Angeles, Alfred Arteaga was raised in Whittier, California. He worked as an editor for *La Raza*, the Partido Raza Unida's journal from Los Angeles, and for *Quarry West*, Raymond Carver's literary journal from Santa Cruz. He is the first Chicano to earn a Master of Fine Arts in creative writing, which he received from Columbia University. He also has a PhD in Literature from the University of California, Santa Cruz. Currently he is an Assistant Professor of English at the University of California, Berkeley where he divides his studies between two renaissances: the English (dead authors) and the Chicano (living authors).